The UNITED STATES PRESIDENTS

Abraham LINCOLN

BreAnn Rumsch

Big Buddy Books

An Imprint of Abdo Publishing

abdopublishing.com

abdopublishing.com

Published by Abdo Publishing, a division of ABDO, PO Box 398166, Minneapolis, Minnesota 55439. Copyright © 2017 by Abdo Consulting Group, Inc. International copyrights reserved in all countries. No part of this book may be reproduced in any form without written permission from the publisher. Big Buddy Books™ is a trademark and logo of Abdo Publishing.

Printed in the United States of America, North Mankato, Minnesota
062016
092016

THIS BOOK CONTAINS
RECYCLED MATERIALS

Design: Sarah DeYoung, Mighty Media, Inc.
Production: Mighty Media, Inc.
Editor: Lauren Kukla
Cover Photograph: Getty Images
Interior Photographs: AP Images (p. 23); Corbis (pp. 6, 11, 13, 17, 25, 27); Getty Images (p. 15);
    iStockphoto (pp. 7, 29); Library of Congress (pp. 5, 9, 19, 21); National Archives (pp. 24, 27)

Cataloging-in-Publication Data

Names: Rumsch, BreAnn, author.
Title: Abraham Lincoln / by BreAnn Rumsch.
Description: Minneapolis, MN : Abdo Publishing, [2017] | Series: United States
    presidents | Includes bibliographical references and index.
Identifiers: LCCN 2015044078 | ISBN 9781680781069 (lib. bdg.) |
    ISBN 9781680775266 (ebook)
Subjects: LCSH: Lincoln, Abraham, 1809-1865--Juvenile literature. 2.
    Presidents--United States--Biography--Juvenile literature. | United States--
    Politics and government--1861-1865--Juvenile literature.
Classification: DDC 973.7/092092 [B]--dc23
LC record available at http://lccn.loc.gov/2015044078

Contents

Abraham Lincoln

Abraham Lincoln was the sixteenth US president. He did not receive much **formal** education. But he loved reading. When Lincoln was just 25, he was elected to the Illinois state **legislature**. Later, he served in the US House of Representatives.

Lincoln became president in 1861. As president, he led the country through the **American Civil War**. Today, many people remember him as the greatest leader in US history.

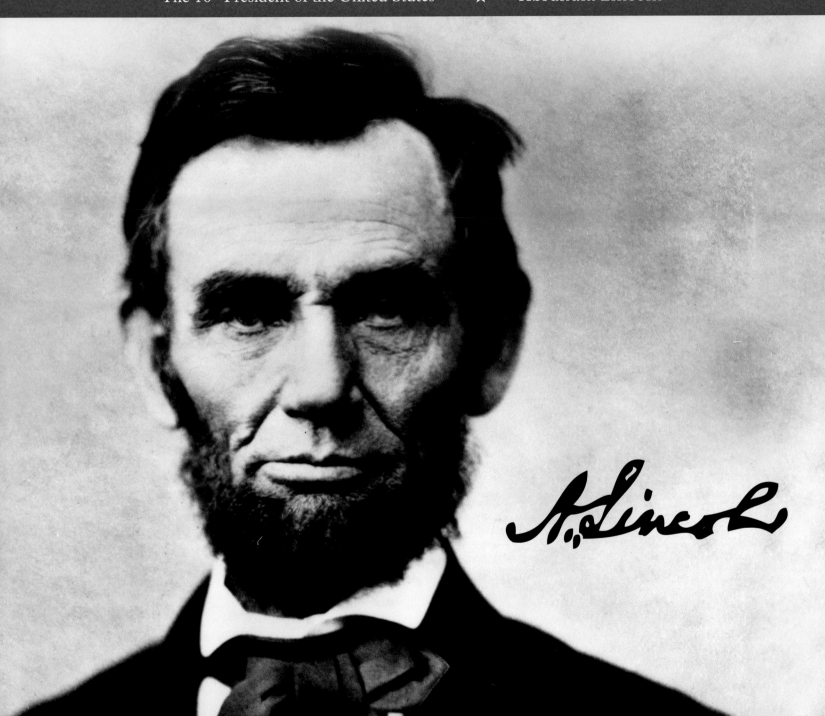

Timeline

1809

On February 12, Abraham Lincoln was born in Hodgenville, Kentucky.

1846

Lincoln won a seat in the US House of Representatives.

1834

Lincoln won a seat in the Illinois state **legislature**.

1860

On November 6, Lincoln was elected the sixteenth US president.

1861

In January, seven Southern states formed the **Confederate States of America**. The Confederacy attacked Fort Sumter on April 12, starting the **American Civil War**.

1863

Lincoln issued the Emancipation Proclamation on January 1.

1865

The American Civil War ended. Abraham Lincoln died on April 15.

A Modest Start

Abraham Lincoln was born in Hodgenville, Kentucky, on February 12, 1809. His parents were Thomas and Nancy Lincoln.

Abraham grew up on farms in Kentucky and Indiana. When he was six years old, Abraham started school.

★ FAST FACTS ★

Born: February 12, 1809

Wife: Mary Ann Todd (1818–1882)

Children: four

Political Party: Republican

Age at Inauguration: 52

Years Served: 1861–1865

Vice Presidents: Hannibal Hamlin, Andrew Johnson

Died: April 15, 1865, age 56

Abraham loved reading whenever he could find time. He read the Bible, *Aesop's Fables*, and *Robinson Crusoe*.

Honest Abe

In 1830, Lincoln's family moved to New Salem, Illinois. Two years later, he decided to run for the Illinois state **legislature**. But before he began, the **Black Hawk War** broke out.

In April, Lincoln joined the Illinois **militia**. He returned home in July. It was just two weeks before the elections. Lincoln received many votes. But he did not win.

In May 1833, Lincoln became New Salem's postmaster. That fall, he also became the deputy county **surveyor**.

Lincoln worked hard as a young man and earned a reputation for honesty. People called him Honest Abe.

Law and Marriage

In 1834, Lincoln again ran for the Illinois state **legislature**. This time he won! He won the next three elections, too. By 1836, Lincoln was a leader of the **Whig Party**.

Lincoln also studied law. He received his law license in 1836. The next year, he moved to Springfield, Illinois.

In 1839, Lincoln met Mary Ann Todd. They married on November 4, 1842. The two had four children. Their names were Robert Todd, Edward, William, and Thomas.

Mary Ann Todd was well educated. Both she and Lincoln loved poetry and shared an interest in politics.

A New Party

In 1846, Lincoln won a seat in the US House of Representatives. He proposed a law to free slaves in Washington, DC. He also tried to ban slavery in other areas. Neither law passed.

Lincoln did not run for reelection. In 1849, he returned to his law practice. Meanwhile, the **Whig Party** died out. The **Republican** Party formed in its place. Lincoln joined this new party in 1856. Then, he helped organize the Illinois branch.

The Lincolns moved into this home in Springfield in May 1844. They lived there for 17 years.

A House Divided

In 1858, the **Republicans nominated** Lincoln for the US Senate. He ran against **Democrat** Stephen A. Douglas. Douglas supported slavery. Lincoln believed the nation could not last if it was **divided** over slavery. Lincoln challenged Douglas to a series of **debates**.

Lincoln lost the US Senate election. But he gained national attention. On May 18, 1860, he was nominated for president. Lincoln won the election on November 6.

Lincoln and Douglas traveled across Illinois debating about slavery.

Road to War

The South's **economy** was based on **agriculture**. Farmers depended on slave labor. They felt Lincoln threatened their way of life.

On December 20, 1860, South Carolina **seceded**. Other Southern states soon followed. Together, they formed the **Confederate States of America**.

Fort Sumter in South Carolina was still under US control. On April 12, 1861, the Confederacy attacked the fort. The **American Civil War** had begun.

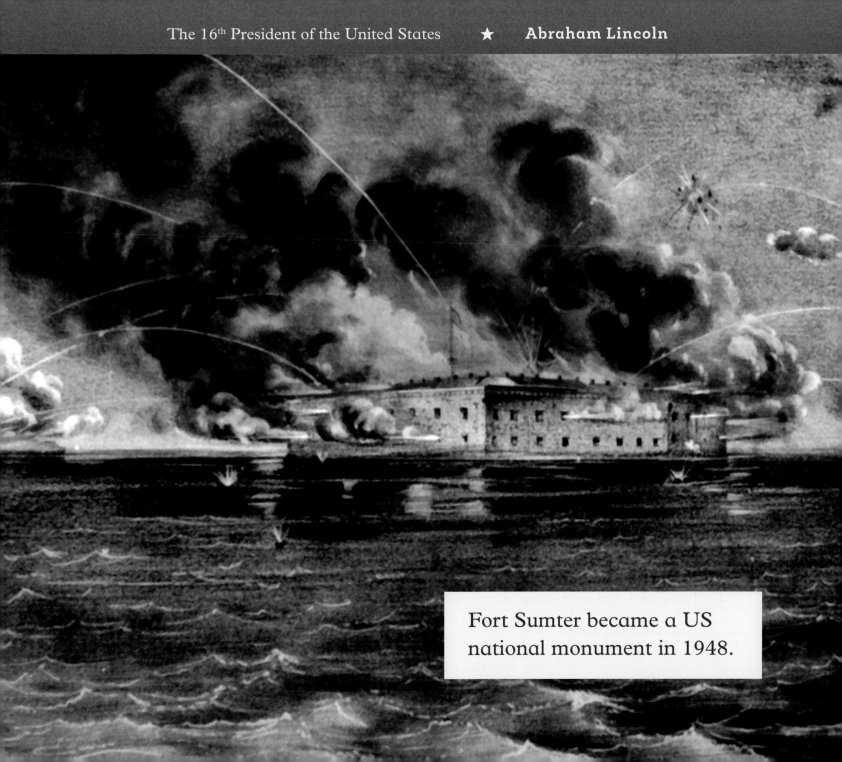

Fort Sumter became a US national monument in 1948.

Wartime Leader

The **Confederacy** won many battles early in the war. But the **Union** struggled to find a good military leader. So Lincoln led the Union himself. In 1862, General Ulysses S. Grant became a Union leader. He defeated the Confederate army in Tennessee. It was the Union's first major **victory** of the war.

SUPREME COURT APPOINTMENTS

Noah H. Swayne: 1862

Samuel Freeman Miller: 1862

David Davis: 1862

Stephen Johnson Field: 1863

Salmon P. Chase: 1864

General Ulysses S. Grant went on to become the eighteenth US president.

Hope for the Future

Lincoln had spent much time thinking about slavery during the war. He felt the US **Constitution** protected slavery where it already existed. But he also believed slavery was wrong.

Lincoln added a new goal to the war. In addition to reuniting the states, he wanted to end slavery. On January 1, 1863, Lincoln issued the Emancipation Proclamation. It announced that all slaves in **Confederate** states were now free.

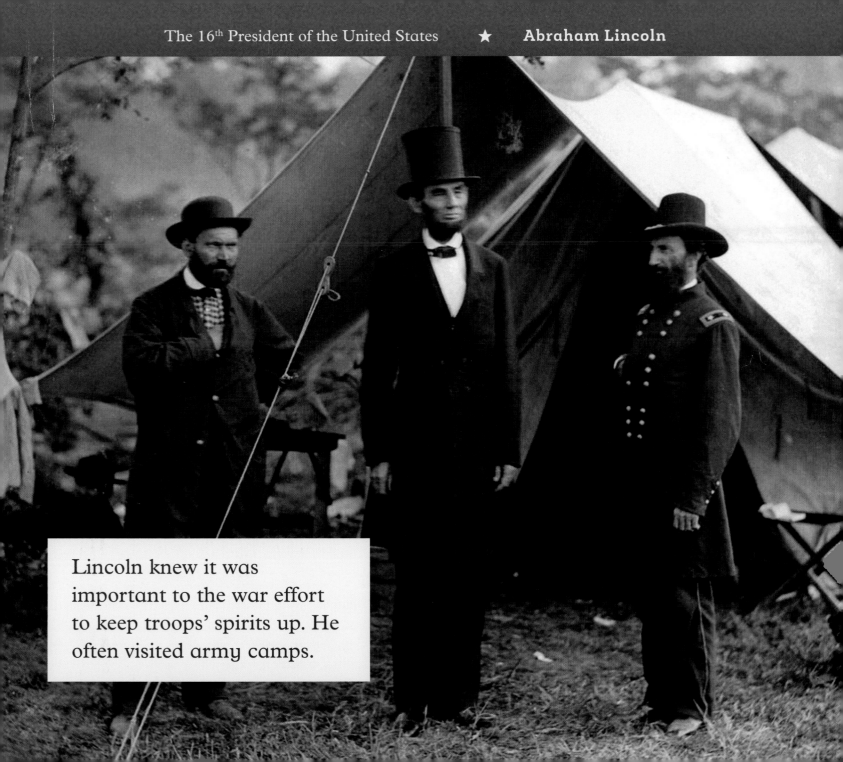

Lincoln knew it was important to the war effort to keep troops' spirits up. He often visited army camps.

In 1863, the North began winning the war. That July, **Union** forces won the Battle of Gettysburg in Pennsylvania. On November 19, the battlefield became a national cemetery. President Lincoln gave a speech during the ceremony. It was known as his Gettysburg Address.

Lincoln's Gettysburg Address was short but powerful. It gave people hope for the future.

PRESIDENT LINCOLN'S CABINET

First Term

March 4, 1861–March 4, 1865

★ **STATE:** William H. Seward

★ **TREASURY:** Salmon P. Chase,
William P. Fessenden (from July 5, 1864)

★ **WAR:** Simon Cameron,
Edwin M. Stanton (from June 20, 1862)

★ **NAVY:** Gideon Welles

★ **ATTORNEY GENERAL:** Edward Bates,
James Speed (from December 5, 1864)

★ **INTERIOR:** Caleb B. Smith,
John P. Usher (from January 8, 1863)

Second Term

March 4, 1865–April 15, 1865

★ **STATE:** William H. Seward

★ **TREASURY:** Hugh McCulloch

★ **WAR:** Edwin M. Stanton

★ **NAVY:** Gideon Welles

★ **ATTORNEY GENERAL:** James Speed

★ **INTERIOR:** John P. Usher

Fighting for Peace

In March 1864, Lincoln gave General Grant command of all US armies. The **Union** won several battles later that year. These **victories** helped Lincoln win reelection in 1864.

Lincoln began his second term in March 1865. On April 9, **Confederate** General Robert E. Lee met with Grant. General Lee **surrendered**. The **American Civil War** was over at last.

★ DID YOU KNOW? ★

Lincoln appears on the nation's one-cent coin and five-dollar bill.

Democrat and former senator Andrew Johnson was Lincoln's running mate for the 1864 election.

Lincoln supported the Thirteenth Amendment. It became part of the US Constitution in December 1865. It banned slavery in the United States.

27

A Tragic Ending

On April 14, 1865, Lincoln went to Ford's Theatre in Washington, DC. He was going to see a play. During the show, John Wilkes Booth snuck into Lincoln's theater box. Booth shot Lincoln. He died the next morning. The nation was shocked and saddened by Lincoln's death.

Lincoln was a strong leader. He led the country through civil war. He worked to end slavery and reunite the nation. These accomplishments made him one of America's most important presidents.

The Lincoln
Memorial in
Washington, DC

Office of the President

Branches of Government

The US government has three branches. They are the executive, legislative, and judicial branches. Each branch has some power over the others. This is called a system of checks and balances.

★ Executive Branch

The executive branch enforces laws. It is made up of the president, the vice president, and the president's cabinet. The president represents the United States around the world. He or she also signs bills into law and leads the military.

★ Legislative Branch

The legislative branch makes laws, maintains the military, and regulates trade. It also has the power to declare war. This branch includes the Senate and the House of Representatives. Together, these two houses form Congress.

★ Judicial Branch

The judicial branch interprets laws. It is made up of district courts, courts of appeals, and the Supreme Court. District courts try cases. Sometimes people disagree with a trial's outcome. Then he or she may appeal. If a court of appeals supports the ruling, a person may appeal to the Supreme Court.

Qualifications for Office

To be president, a candidate must be at least 35 years old. The person must be a natural-born US citizen. He or she must also have lived in the United States for at least 14 years.

Electoral College

The US presidential election is an indirect election. Voters from each state choose electors. These electors represent their state in the Electoral College. Each elector has one electoral vote. Electors cast their vote for the candidate with the highest number of votes from people in their state. A candidate must receive the majority of Electoral College votes to win.

Term of Office

Each president may be elected to two four-year terms. The presidential election is held on the Tuesday after the first Monday in November. The president is sworn in on January 20 of the following year. At that time, he or she takes the oath of office. It states:

> I do solemnly swear (or affirm) that I will faithfully execute the office of President of the United States, and will to the best of my ability, preserve, protect and defend the Constitution of the United States.

31

Line of Succession

The Presidential Succession Act of 1947 states who becomes president if the president cannot serve. The vice president is first in the line. Next are the Speaker of the House and the President Pro Tempore of the Senate. It may happen that none of these individuals is able to serve. Then the office falls to the president's cabinet members. They would take office in the order in which each department was created:

Secretary of State

Secretary of the Treasury

Secretary of Defense

Attorney General

Secretary of the Interior

Secretary of Agriculture

Secretary of Commerce

Secretary of Labor

Secretary of Health and Human Services

Secretary of Housing and Urban Development

Secretary of Transportation

Secretary of Energy

Secretary of Education

Secretary of Veterans Affairs

Secretary of Homeland Security

Benefits

★ While in office, the president receives a salary. It is $400,000 per year. He or she lives in the White House. The president also has 24-hour Secret Service protection.

★ The president may travel on a Boeing 747 jet. This special jet is called Air Force One. It can hold 70 passengers. It has kitchens, a dining room, sleeping areas, and more. Air Force One can fly halfway around the world before needing to refuel. It can even refuel in flight!

★ When the president travels by car, he or she uses Cadillac One. It is a Cadillac Deville that has been modified. The car has heavy armor and communications systems. The president may even take Cadillac One along when visiting other countries.

★ The president also travels on a helicopter. It is called Marine One. It may also be taken along when the president visits other countries.

★ Sometimes the president needs to get away with family and friends. Camp David is the official presidential retreat. It is located in Maryland. The US Navy maintains the retreat. The US Marine Corps keeps it secure. The camp offers swimming, tennis, golf, and hiking.

★ When the president leaves office, he or she receives lifetime Secret Service protection. He or she also receives a yearly pension of $203,700. The former president also receives money for office space, supplies, and staff.

PRESIDENTS AND THEIR TERMS

PRESIDENT	PARTY	TOOK OFFICE	LEFT OFFICE	TERMS SERVED	VICE PRESIDENT
George Washington	None	April 30, 1789	March 4, 1797	Two	John Adams
John Adams	Federalist	March 4, 1797	March 4, 1801	One	Thomas Jefferson
Thomas Jefferson	Democratic-Republican	March 4, 1801	March 4, 1809	Two	Aaron Burr, George Clinton
James Madison	Democratic-Republican	March 4, 1809	March 4, 1817	Two	George Clinton, Elbridge Gerry
James Monroe	Democratic-Republican	March 4, 1817	March 4, 1825	Two	Daniel D. Tompkins
John Quincy Adams	Democratic-Republican	March 4, 1825	March 4, 1829	One	John C. Calhoun
Andrew Jackson	Democrat	March 4, 1829	March 4, 1837	Two	John C. Calhoun, Martin Van Buren
Martin Van Buren	Democrat	March 4, 1837	March 4, 1841	One	Richard M. Johnson
William H. Harrison	Whig	March 4, 1841	April 4, 1841	Died During First Term	John Tyler
John Tyler	Whig	April 6, 1841	March 4, 1845	Completed Harrison's Term	Office Vacant
James K. Polk	Democrat	March 4, 1845	March 4, 1849	One	George M. Dallas
Zachary Taylor	Whig	March 5, 1849	July 9, 1850	Died During First Term	Millard Fillmore

PRESIDENT	PARTY	TOOK OFFICE	LEFT OFFICE	TERMS SERVED	VICE PRESIDENT
Millard Fillmore	Whig	July 10, 1850	March 4, 1853	Completed Taylor's Term	Office Vacant
Franklin Pierce	Democrat	March 4, 1853	March 4, 1857	One	William R.D. King
James Buchanan	Democrat	March 4, 1857	March 4, 1861	One	John C. Breckinridge
Abraham Lincoln	Republican	March 4, 1861	April 15, 1865	Served One Term, Died During Second Term	Hannibal Hamlin, Andrew Johnson
Andrew Johnson	Democrat	April 15, 1865	March 4, 1869	Completed Lincoln's Second Term	Office Vacant
Ulysses S. Grant	Republican	March 4, 1869	March 4, 1877	Two	Schuyler Colfax, Henry Wilson
Rutherford B. Hayes	Republican	March 3, 1877	March 4, 1881	One	William A. Wheeler
James A. Garfield	Republican	March 4, 1881	September 19, 1881	Died During First Term	Chester Arthur
Chester Arthur	Republican	September 20, 1881	March 4, 1885	Completed Garfield's Term	Office Vacant
Grover Cleveland	Democrat	March 4, 1885	March 4, 1889	One	Thomas A. Hendricks
Benjamin Harrison	Republican	March 4, 1889	March 4, 1893	One	Levi P. Morton
Grover Cleveland	Democrat	March 4, 1893	March 4, 1897	One	Adlai E. Stevenson
William McKinley	Republican	March 4, 1897	September 14, 1901	Served One Term, Died During Second Term	Garret A. Hobart, Theodore Roosevelt

PRESIDENT	PARTY	TOOK OFFICE	LEFT OFFICE	TERMS SERVED	VICE PRESIDENT
Theodore Roosevelt	Republican	September 14, 1901	March 4, 1909	Completed McKinley's Second Term, Served One Term	Office Vacant, Charles Fairbanks
William Taft	Republican	March 4, 1909	March 4, 1913	One	James S. Sherman
Woodrow Wilson	Democrat	March 4, 1913	March 4, 1921	Two	Thomas R. Marshall
Warren G. Harding	Republican	March 4, 1921	August 2, 1923	Died During First Term	Calvin Coolidge
Calvin Coolidge	Republican	August 3, 1923	March 4, 1929	Completed Harding's Term, Served One Term	Office Vacant, Charles Dawes
Herbert Hoover	Republican	March 4, 1929	March 4, 1933	One	Charles Curtis
Franklin D. Roosevelt	Democrat	March 4, 1933	April 12, 1945	Served Three Terms, Died During Fourth Term	John Nance Garner, Henry A. Wallace, Harry S. Truman
Harry S. Truman	Democrat	April 12, 1945	January 20, 1953	Completed Roosevelt's Fourth Term, Served One Term	Office Vacant, Alben Barkley
Dwight D. Eisenhower	Republican	January 20, 1953	January 20, 1961	Two	Richard Nixon
John F. Kennedy	Democrat	January 20, 1961	November 22, 1963	Died During First Term	Lyndon B. Johnson
Lyndon B. Johnson	Democrat	November 22, 1963	January 20, 1969	Completed Kennedy's Term, Served One Term	Office Vacant, Hubert H. Humphrey
Richard Nixon	Republican	January 20, 1969	August 9, 1974	Completed First Term, Resigned During Second Term	Spiro T. Agnew, Gerald Ford

PRESIDENT	PARTY	TOOK OFFICE	LEFT OFFICE	TERMS SERVED	VICE PRESIDENT
Gerald Ford	Republican	August 9, 1974	January 20, 1977	Completed Nixon's Second Term	Nelson A. Rockefeller
Jimmy Carter	Democrat	January 20, 1977	January 20, 1981	One	Walter Mondale
Ronald Reagan	Republican	January 20, 1981	January 20, 1989	Two	George H.W. Bush
George H.W. Bush	Republican	January 20, 1989	January 20, 1993	One	Dan Quayle
Bill Clinton	Democrat	January 20, 1993	January 20, 2001	Two	Al Gore
George W. Bush	Republican	January 20, 2001	January 20, 2009	Two	Dick Cheney
Barack Obama	Democrat	January 20, 2009	January 20, 2017	Two	Joe Biden

"I leave you hoping that the lamp of liberty will burn in your bosoms until there shall no longer be a doubt that all men are created free and equal." Abraham Lincoln

★ WRITE TO THE PRESIDENT ★

You may write to the president at:
The White House
1600 Pennsylvania Avenue NW
Washington, DC 20500

You may e-mail the president at:
comments@whitehouse.gov

37

Glossary

agriculture—farming.

American Civil War—the war between the Northern and Southern states from 1861 to 1865.

Black Hawk War—a brief war between the United States and Native Americans fought between April and August 1832.

Confederate States of America—the group of 11 Southern states that declared independency during the American Civil War. It is also called the Confederacy.

Constitution—the laws that govern the United States.

debate—a planned discussion or argument about a question or topic, often held in public.

Democrat—a member of the Democratic political party.

divide—to separate into two parts.

economy—the way that a country produces, sells, and buys goods and services.

formal—official.

legislature—a group of people with the power to make or change laws.

militia (muh-LIH-shuh)—people who help the army in times of need, they are not soldiers.

nominate—to name as a possible winner.

Republican—a member of the Republican political party.

secede—to officially withdraw from a group or organization.

surrender—to give up.

surveyor—someone whose job is to measure land.

Union—the Northern states that remained part of the United States during the American Civil War.

victory—a win.

Whig Party—a US political party active between 1834 and 1854.

★ WEBSITES ★

To learn more about the US Presidents, visit **booklinks.abdopublishing.com**. These links are routinely monitored and updated to provide the most current information available.

Index